SINGuini

Noodling Around
with Silly Songs

Heather Stenner
Cheryl Miller Thurston

Requests for special permission should be addressed to:

Cottonwood Press, Inc.
109-B Cameron Drive
Fort Collins, Colorado 80525

Email: cottonwood@cottonwoodpress.com
Phone: 1-800-864-4297
Fax: 970-204-0761
www.cottonwoodpress.com

ISBN 1-877673-69-2

Printed in the United States of America

Cover Illustration © 2006 Joyce M. Turley, Dixon Cove Design

For Emma

Table of Contents

Introduction

We admit it. The goofy songs in *SINGuini* meet no lofty educational goals. They are meant for fun—pure and simple fun. Oh, kids may learn a bit about music as they learn the songs, but that's not the point. The point is for them to just enjoy singing.

While silly songs are common for children in pre-school and primary grades, humor often disappears in music for older kids. It shouldn't. Intermediate, middle school, and junior high students can have just as much fun as anyone else with a bit of goofiness in their music.

Older students love the tongue-twisting madness of "Impossible to Sing Song," and they laugh (and groan) at "Snot Is Not the Proper Subject for a Song." They love the rhythmic challenge of "Ugh" and "Boom Snap Clap." They appreciate parodies like "My Bonnie Went in for a Face Lift" and "On Top of a Bald Guy." Long after they have outgrown "Itsy Bitsy Spider," they enjoy "Itsy Bitsy Down the Drain."

Try *SINGuini* songs in the classroom, at camp, with youth groups or with your own kids in the car or around the kitchen table. If you lead an adult singing group, you might even like to try some of the songs with them. It's good for grown-ups to smile, too!

Using SINGuini. *SINGuini* is divided into four sections:

- The first section shows just the basics—the melody and lyrics. If you are a teacher or group leader, these short melodies are easy to photocopy to hand out to your students, for your own classroom use.
- If you need simple piano accompaniment, turn to the "Accompaniment" section, page 89.
- If you want just the words, turn to the "Lyrics at a Glance" section, page 191.
- If you are looking for songs with certain specifications, check "Time Signatures and Key Signatures at a Glance," page 204.

Enjoy! Both of us grew up in families that sang. Some of our strongest and fondest memories of childhood are wrapped around silly songs like "I'm Being Eaten By a Boa Constrictor" and "There Was an Old Lady Who Swallowed a Fly." Singing songs was part of our family fabric, and that's why developing new songs has been such a joy for us. We hope that some of the songs in *SINGuini* make their way into the memories of a new generation.

Heather Stenner and Cheryl Miller Thurston

MELODY ONLY

Songs to the Tune of Old Favorites

Bill Loves Jill

Lyrics by Cheryl Miller Thurston
Arr. by Heather Stenner

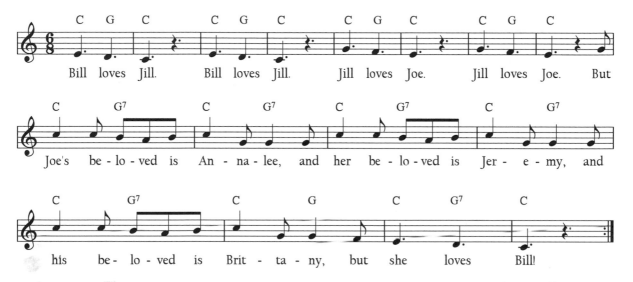

See page 91 for accompaniment.

2nd verse:

Ann loves Dan.
Ann loves Dan.
Dan loves Dee.
Dan loves Dee.
But Dee's beloved is Anthony,
and his beloved is Bethany,
and her beloved is Timothy,
But he loves Ann!

Love gone wrong is the subject of this song, sung to the tune of "Three Blind Mice."

My Bonnie Went in for a Face Lift

Lyrics by Cheryl Miller Thurston
Arr. by Heather Stenner

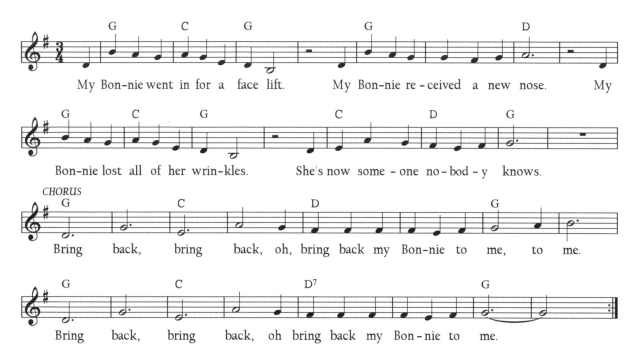

My Bon-nie went in for a face lift. My Bon-nie re-ceived a new nose. My

Bon-nie lost all of her wrin-kles. She's now some - one no-bod-y knows.

CHORUS

Bring back, bring back, oh, bring back my Bon-nie to me, to me.

Bring back, bring back, oh bring back my Bon-nie to me.

See page 92 for accompaniment.

2nd verse:

My Bonnie lost all of her chins, and
The pouches below both her eyes.
Her skin is now smooth as a baby's—
She's nobody I recognize.

Repeat chorus.

Stand up and then sit down quickly whenever you sing the words "My Bonnie."

Z-Y-X

Lyrics by Cheryl Miller Thurston
Arr. by Heather Stenner

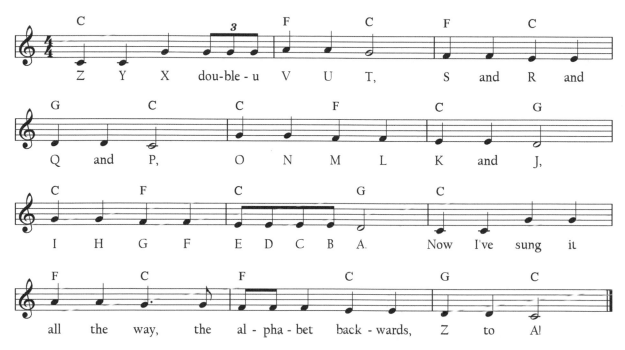

See page 94 for accompaniment.

It's tricky to sing the alphabet backwards! Sing this to the tune of "Twinkle, Twinkle, Little Star."

Oh, My Darling Frankensteen

Lyrics by Cheryl Miller Thurston
Arr. by Heather Stenner

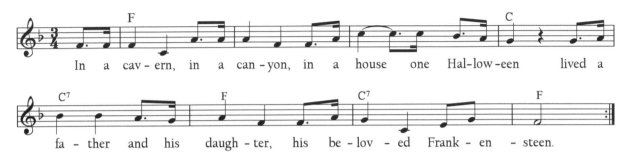

In a cav-ern, in a can-yon, in a house one Hal-low-een lived a fa-ther and his daugh-ter, his be-lov-ed Frank-en-steen.

See page 95 for accompaniment.

More verses:

He had built her in his lab with
a bizarre and big machine.
And he loved her very dearly,
his beloved Frankensteen.

She was not a natural beauty.
She wore shoes, size seventeen.
All her hair was made of barbed wire,
and her face was olive green.

Both her eyes were bolted on with
lots of chicken wire between.
What had once been part of fencing
was a nose on Frankensteen.

He decided she should marry,
but the men around were mean.
Not a one would even talk to
his beloved Frankensteen.

So he went into his lab to
his bizarre and big machine,
and he built a future husband
for his darling Frankensteen.

Plugged him in and called his daughter
and said, "Darling, meet Eugene."
And she sighed to see the cutest
guy she'd ever, ever seen.

It was instant love for both, and
sparks were flying at the scene.
But alas, there was some gas, and
they were blown to smithereens.

Oh, his darling, oh his darling,
Oh, his darling Frankensteen.
She is lost and gone forever,
but at least she's with Eugene.

"Oh, My Darling Clementine" couldn't swim. Poor Frankensteen has a different set of problems.

On Top of a Bald Guy

Lyrics by Cheryl Miller Thurston
Arr. by Heather Stenner

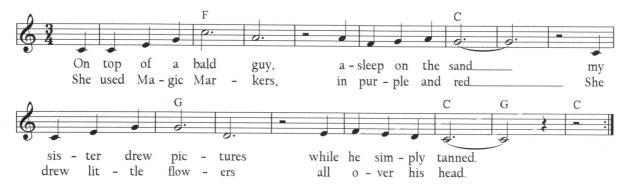

On top of a bald guy, a-sleep on the sand_____ my
She used Ma-gic Mar-kers, in pur-ple and red_____ She

sis - ter drew pic - tures while he sim - ply tanned.
drew lit - tle flow - ers all o - ver his head.

See page 96 for accompaniment.

More verses:

She added a mustache
right under his nose,
and there on his forehead,
she painted a rose.

And when he turned over
and started to snore,
she added some tulips
and daisies and more.

But when the guy snorted
and started to wake,
my sister decided,
"Hey, time for a break."

She went in the ocean.
I stayed in my chair
to watch the old bald guy
with flowers for hair.

I couldn't help laughing.
He looked so confused.
He wondered why others
were looking amused.

He borrowed a mirror
and saw his new hair.
He saw all the flowers
and me sitting there.

He jumped to conclusions.
He started to growl.
I jumped to my feet as
he jumped from his towel.

I ran to the ocean.
He ran after me.
My sister just smiled as
I jumped in the sea.

I'm still treading water.
My future is grim.
But I sure am happy
That bald guy can't swim!

Everyone knows "On Top of Spaghetti," the parody of "On Top of Old Smoky." Here's a newer twist.

My Bike Has a Flat Tire

Lyrics by Cheryl Miller Thurston
Arr. by Heather Stenner

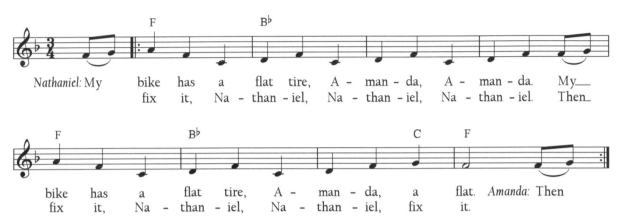

Nathaniel: My bike has a flat tire, A - man - da, A - man - da. My___
fix it, Na - than - iel, Na - than - iel, Na - than - iel. Then___

bike has a flat tire, A - man - da, a flat. *Amanda:* Then
fix it, Na - than - iel, Na - than - iel, fix it.

See page 97 for accompaniment.

With this updated version "There's a Hole in My Bucket," boys sing Nathaniel's part, and girls sing Amanda's.

More verses:

Nathaniel: But how should I fix it, Amanda, Amanda?
             But how should I fix it, Amanda, but how?

Amanda: With a bike pump, Nathaniel, Nathaniel, Nathaniel.
             With a bike pump, Nathaniel, Nathaniel, a pump.

Nathaniel: But the pump handle's broken, Amanda, Amanda.
             But the pump handle's broken. Amanda, it's broke.

Amanda: Then glue it, Nathaniel, Nathaniel, Nathaniel.
             Then glue it, Nathaniel, Nathaniel, glue it.

Nathaniel: I'm all out of glue, Amanda, Amanda.
             I'm all out of glue, Amanda, no glue.

Amanda: Then buy some, Nathaniel, Nathaniel, Nathaniel.
             Then buy some, Nathaniel, Nathaniel, buy some.

Nathaniel: But where should I buy it, Amanda, Amanda?
             But where should I buy it, Amanda, but where?

Amanda: At WalMart, Nathaniel, Nathaniel, Nathaniel.
             At WalMart, Nathaniel, Nathaniel, WalMart.

Nathaniel: But how should I get there, Amanda, Amanda?
             But how should I get there, Amanda, but how?

Amanda: On your bi-ike, Nathaniel, Nathaniel, Nathaniel.
             On your bi-ike, Nathaniel, Nathaniel, your bike.

Nathaniel: My bike has a flat tire, Amanda, Amanda!
             My bike has a flat tire, Amanda, a flat!!!!!

Mary Possessed a Petite
Offspring of a Ewe

Lyrics by Cheryl Miller Thurston
Arr. by Heather Stenner

It caused the stu-dents to show a-muse-ment and

frol - ic and ca-vort, fro - lic and ca-vort, frol - ic and ca - vort. It

caused the stu-dents to show a - muse - ment and frol - ic and ca - vort, to ob -

serve the off - spring of a ewe at an in - sti - tu - tion of learn - ing.

See page 98 for accompaniment.

It's tricky to get all the words in when singing this annoyingly formal version of "Mary Had a Little Lamb."

A Spaceship Landed

Lyrics by Cheryl Miller Thurston
Arr. by Heather Stenner

See page 99 for accompaniment.

More verses:

Oh, the top popped open.
They all came out.
They had green ears
and purple snouts.
Oh, the top popped open.
They all came out.
They had green ears
and purple snouts.
I won't go back there anymore.

Chorus

Oh, they waved their arms.
They had sixteen.
They looked dressed up
for Halloween.
They waved their arms.
They had sixteen.
They looked dressed up
for Halloween.
I won't go back there anymore.

Chorus

Oh, they held up signs
that made no sense.
They opened packs
and pitched some tents.
They held up signs
that made no sense.
They opened packs
and pitched some tents.
I won't go back there anymore.

Chorus

Oh, it's been a year.
They haven't left.
They ate my lawn.
There's nothing left.
It's been a year.
They haven't left.
They ate my lawn.
There's nothing left.
I won't go back there anymore.

Chorus

Oh, they sing all night.
They never miss.
They sing a song
that goes like this:
Ziddle-op-dorp-giddle-op,
ziddle-iddle-ay.
Ziddle-op-dorp-giddle-op,
ziddle-iddle-ay.
Ziddle-op-dorp-dorp,
ziddle-iddle-iddle-ay.

This echo song is based on an old standard called "Oh, You Can't Get to Heaven."

I Am the Very Model of a Perfect Son or Daughter

Lyrics by Cheryl Miller Thurston
Arr. by Heather Stenner

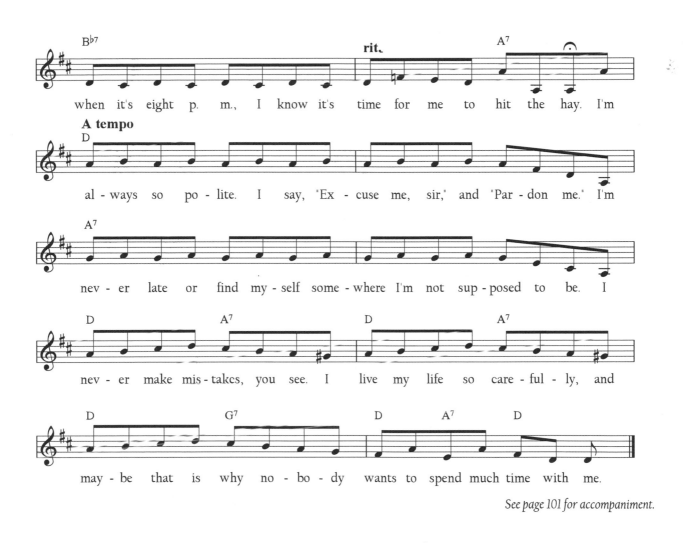

when it's eight p. m., I know it's time for me to hit the hay. I'm
al - ways so po - lite. I say, "Ex - cuse me, sir," and "Par - don me." I'm
nev - er late or find my - self some - where I'm not sup - posed to be. I
nev - er make mis - takes, you see. I live my life so care - ful - ly, and
may - be that is why no - bo - dy wants to spend much time with me.

See page 101 for accompaniment.

This song about someone who does everything right is based on a Gilbert and Sullivan song called "Modern Major General," written more than 125 years ago.

There's a House in the Middle of the Town

Lyrics by Cheryl Miller Thurston
Arr. by Heather Stenner

See page 105 for accompaniment.

More verses:

3. There's a child in the chair in the house in the middle of the town.
There's a child in the chair in the house in the middle of the town.
There's a child. There's a child.
There's a child in the chair in the house in the middle of the town.

4. There's a bib on the child in the chair in the house in the middle of the town.
There's a bib on the child in the chair in the house in the middle of the town.
There's a bib. There's a bib.
There's a bib on the child in the chair in the house in the middle of the town.

5. There's a drip on the bib on the child in the chair in the house in the middle of the town.
There's a drip on the bib on the child in the chair in the house in the middle of the town.
There's a drip. There's a drip.
There's a drip on the bib on the child in the chair in the house in the middle of the town.

6. There's a fly on the drip on the bib on the child in the chair in the house in the middle of the town.
There's a fly on the drip on the bib on the child in the chair in the house in the middle of the town.
There's a fly. There's a fly.
There's a fly on the drip on the bib on the child in the chair in the house in the middle of the town.

7. There's a flea on the fly on the drip on the bib on the child in the chair in the house in the middle of the town.
There's a flea on the fly on the drip on the bib on the child in the chair in the house in the middle of the town.
There's a flea. There's a flea.
There's a flea on the fly on the drip on the bib on the child in the chair in the house in the middle of the town.

8. There's a speck on the flea on the fly on the drip on the bib on the child in the chair in the house in the middle of the town.
There's a speck on the flea on the fly on the drip on the bib on the child in the chair in the house in the middle of the town.
There's a speck. There's a speck.
There's a speck on the flea on the fly on the drip on the bib on the child in the chair in the house in the middle of the town.

"There's a Hole at the Bottom of the Sea" moves to the city in this new version of an old song.

For more "To the Tune Of" songs, see also:

Alexander's Outside Eating Bugs, page 38
Cell Phone Song, page 40
Yes!, page 62
Picking up a Pepperoni Pizza, page 78

Story Songs

Boa Constrictor

Lyrics by Cheryl Miller Thurston
Music by Heather Stenner

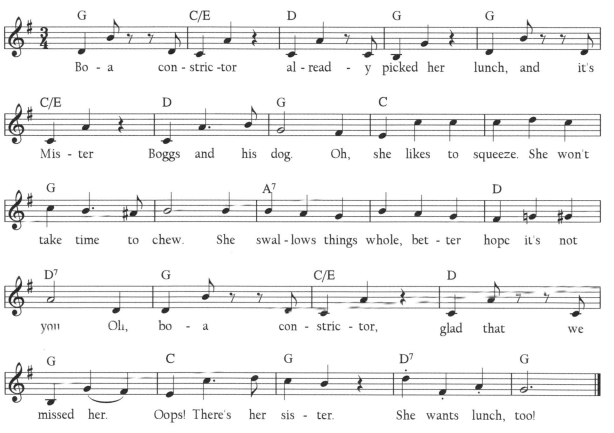

Bo - a con - stric -tor al - read - y picked her lunch, and it's
Mis - ter Boggs and his dog. Oh, she likes to squeeze. She won't
take time to chew. She swal -lows things whole, bet - ter hope it's not
you Oh, bo - a con - stric - tor, glad that we
missed her. Oops! There's her sis - ter. She wants lunch, too!

See page 107 for accompaniment.

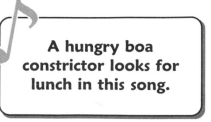

A hungry boa constrictor looks for lunch in this song.

Whiffling, Waffling Will

Lyrics by Cheryl Miller Thurston
Music by Heather Stenner

See page 109 for accompaniment.

More verses:

I asked my boyfriend to go to the show.
He said, "Yes, maybe no, maybe yes, maybe no."
He couldn't decide if he wanted to go,
so he said, "Flip a coin, 'cause I really don't know."

Whiffling, waffling, whiffling Will.
Whiffling, waffling, whiffling Will.
Whiffling, waffling, whiffling Will.
Whiffling, waffling, whiffling Will.

I asked my boyfriend to go for a ride.
He said, "Yes, maybe no, maybe yes, maybe no."
I got out my bike, but he couldn't decide,
so I said, "I have had it, and this is 'Goodbye.'"

Whiffling, waffling, whiffling Will.
Whiffling, waffling, whiffling Will.
Whiffling, waffling, whiffling Will.
Whiffling, waffling, whiffling Will.

Some people just can't make up their minds. That doesn't mean others have to put up with them forever!

Victor Vacuumed

Lyrics by Cheryl Miller Thurston
Music by Heather Stenner

Though the pup - py was - n't hap - py, Vic - tor did - n't care.

Vic - tor vac - uumed up his sis - ter, crawl - ing by his chair.

Though his sis - ter was - n't hap - py, Vic - tor did - n't care.

Vic - tor's sis - ter crawled back out and stood on Vic - tor's chair.

Then she vac - uumed Vic - tor up, and NOW Vic - tor cares!

See page 111 for accompaniment.

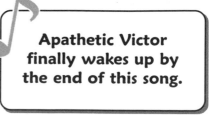

Apathetic Victor finally wakes up by the end of this song.

Peas

Lyrics by Cheryl Miller Thurston
Music by Heather Stenner

See page 114 for accompaniment.

3rd verse:

"I'd like to order now," said my friend.
"I won't be asking what you will recommend.
I think that I will have some of these."
He pointed to the picture of a bowl of peas.

"Oh, no, sir, if you please,
I have promised all our peas.
Oh, no, sir, now it seems all that I can give you, sir, is
beans and beans and beans and beans and beans. Just beans!"

Most of us are frustrated when someone else insists on making decisions for us. What if your decisions were being made by your waiter?

Alexander's Outside Eating Bugs

Lyrics by Cheryl Miller Thurston
Arr. by Heather Stenner

mag - got and a mil - li - pede, a ter - mite and a beet - le and a

crick - et and a cen - ti - pede, and now he's got a spit - tle - bug, and

now he's got a ba - by slu - ug! Al - ex - an - der's out - side eat - ing bugs.

I am in - side feel - ing kind of yuck - y.

And I won - der, "Must he be so darned dis - gust - ing?"

Eeeew! *Spoken:* Argh. Ahh. Urp. Ugh. (etc.) I'm sick!

See page 116 for accompaniment.

Some listeners will recognize this classic tune as "Dance of the Reed Flutes" from the Nutcracker Ballet. It was popularized in the Disney animated film, Fantasia. The words in this version are entirely new.

Cell Phone Song

Lyrics by Cheryl Miller Thurston
Arr. by Heather Stenner

think he'd have the time to get some gas, but, yes, when he got home he would be

sure to cut the grass. We thought we knew that he was through when peo - ple

yelled and pop-corn flew! Then he put his daugh-ter on so she could say "Hi!" too.

See page 120 for accompaniment.

♪ **Who hasn't been annoyed by cell phones ringing at the wrong time? The tune is an old song called "Funiculi, Funicula."**

Don't Wanna Be a Couch Potato

Lyrics by Cheryl Miller Thurston
Music by Heather Stenner

and when a six ton truck drove through his house, that
fel - la did - n't ev - en look up! Don't wan - na be a
couch po - ta - to, a lump on a sof - a or bed. Don't wan - na be a
couch po - ta - to, soft as a loaf - a bread. I don't wan - na be a
couch po - ta - to. No, not me! It's de - test - a - ble to be a
veg - 'ta - ble. Not me. It's de-
test - a - ble to be a veg - 'ta - ble. Not me.

See page 124 for accompaniment.

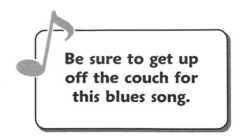

Be sure to get up off the couch for this blues song.

Bill Bought a Backpack Bigger than Bill

Lyrics by Cheryl Miller Thurston
Music by Heather Stenner

See page 128 for accompaniment.

More verses:

Well, someone finally happened by.
It was his sister Loralei.
She looked at him and then she laughed,
And laughed and laughed and laughed and laughed.

She got her car and got a rope,
Said, "I'll help you, you lit-tle dope."
She tied that rope 'round him where he lay
And one end on the Chevrolet.

Chorus

Well, Loralei said, "Now hold on tight.
I will get you up to-oo-night.
She got in the car and stepped on the gas—
Pulled poor Bill up off his... *(pause)*...back!

His back, back, back, back, off of his back,
Pulled poor Bi-ill up off of his back.
His back, back, back, back, off of his back.
She saved poor Bill from his pack attack!

Chorus

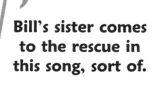

**Bill's sister comes
to the rescue in
this song, sort of.**

45

For more "Story" songs, see also:

Miscellaneous Fun

Never Hug a Hibble

Lyrics by Cheryl Miller Thurston
Music by Heather Stenner

See page 130 for accompaniment.

More verses:

Never bite a bibble in a bibble babble borper.
Never bite a bibble in a bibble babble borp (etc.).

Never squeeze a squibble in a squibble squabble squorper.
Never squeeze a squibble in a squibble squabble squorp (etc.).

Never try a tribble in a tribble trabble trorper.
Never try a tribble in a tribble trabble trorp (etc.).

(Other verb ideas: grab, race, pat, etc.)

You can change this song endlessly by substituting different one-syllable verbs.

Her Poodle Likes Noodles

Lyrics by Cheryl Miller Thurston
Music by Heather Stenner

cor - ru - gat - ed box - es._____ Her chow -chow likes bow -wow - ing

all day long, and some - times her box - er likes shorts._____

— Her schnau - zer likes trou - sers. Her aire - dale likes

planes, and her grey - hound likes bus - es, of course!

See page 131 for accompaniment.

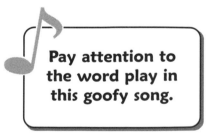

Pay attention to the word play in this goofy song.

I Like Your Singin'

Lyrics by Cheryl Miller Thurston
Music by Heather Stenner

sing - in'. Sing - in' all day long. Oh, I love to

hear you sing, 'Flip - flop - di - flong." Don't e - ven care if your

song is too long_____

I like your sing - in'. I like your song. I like your

sing - in'. Sing - in' all day long.

rit. _ _ _ _ _ _ _ _ _ _ _ _ _ _

See page 134 for accompaniment.

This song gives you permission to break some "rules."

Surfing Polka Band

Lyrics by Cheryl Miller Thurston
Music by Heather Stenner

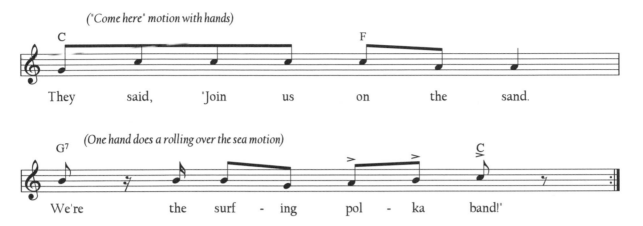

("Come here" motion with hands)

C   F

They   said,   "Join   us   on   the   sand.

(One hand does a rolling over the sea motion)

G⁷

We're   the   surf - ing   pol - ka   band!"

See page 138 for accompaniment.

This song includes hand motions to go with each phrase. Sing the song nine times. The first time through, sing all the phrases and do all the hand motions. The second time through, leave out the first phrase, but do the hand motions. The next time, leave out the first and second phrases, but do the hand motions. Continue in this manner, leaving out a phrase each time. By the end of the song, you will use no words at all—only hand motions!

Impossible to Sing Song

Lyrics by Cheryl Miller Thurston
Music by Heather Stenner

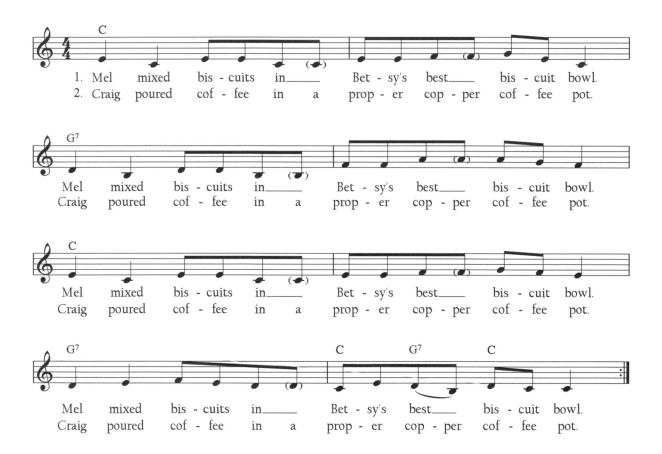

1. Mel mixed bis - cuits in___ Bet - sy's best___ bis - cuit bowl.
2. Craig poured cof - fee in a prop - er cop - per cof - fee pot.

Mel mixed bis - cuits in___ Bet - sy's best___ bis - cuit bowl.
Craig poured cof - fee in a prop - er cop - per cof - fee pot.

Mel mixed bis - cuits in___ Bet - sy's best___ bis - cuit bowl.
Craig poured cof - fee in a prop - er cop - per cof - fee pot.

Mel mixed bis - cuits in___ Bet - sy's best___ bis - cuit bowl.
Craig poured cof - fee in a prop - er cop - per cof - fee pot.

See page 140 for accompaniment.

This song really, truly IS impossible to sing. The fun is in trying! For an added challenge, sing it faster and faster each time through.

Ugh!

Lyrics by Cheryl Miller Thurston
Music by Heather Stenner

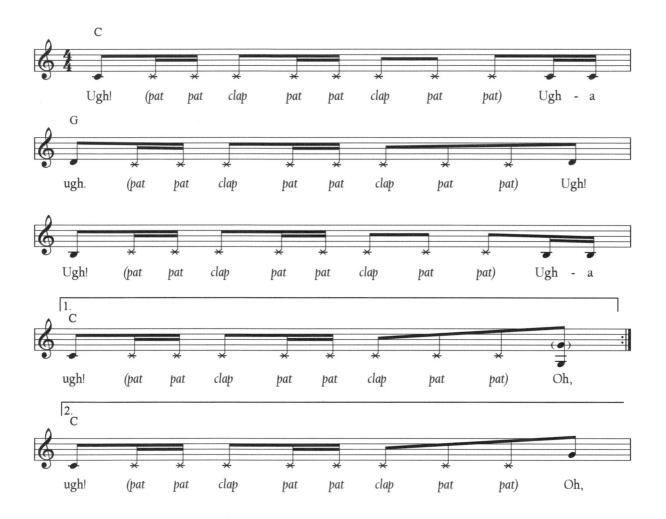

Motions

On "pat," alternate between patting your left and right leg.
On "clap," clap your hands together.

During this section, keep a stomping beat in your feet.

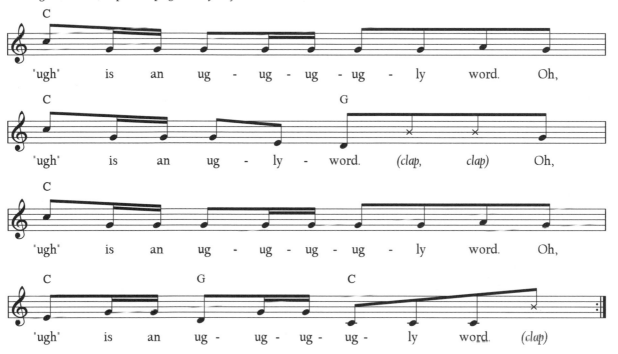

See page 142 for accompaniment.

Sing this faster, each time through. The rhythm becomes more and more challenging, the faster you go. Keep repeating, until exhausted!

This Is a Boring Song

Lyrics by Cheryl Miller Thurston
Music by Heather Stenner

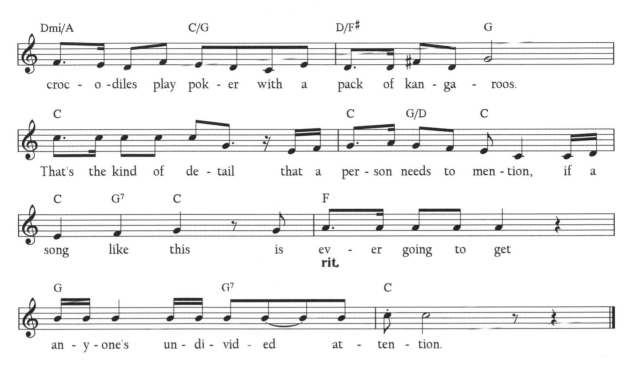

croc - o -diles play pok - er with a pack of kan - ga - roos.

That's the kind of de - tail that a per - son needs to men - tion, if a

song like this is ev - er going to get

rit.

an - y - one's un - di - vid - ed at - ten - tion.

See page 145 for accompaniment.

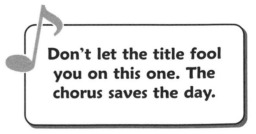

Don't let the title fool you on this one. The chorus saves the day.

Yes!

Lyrics by Cheryl Miller Thurston
Arr. by Heather Stenner

will, I will, I will, I will. Oh, yes! Yes! Yes! O-

kay. O - kay. Uh - huh, uh - huh, and yup. I

will, I will, I will, I will, I will. Thumbs up!

See page 148 for accompaniment.

Whenever you're feeling grumpy or negative, try this song for a change in attitude. It's to the tune of Schumann's "The Happy Farmer."

Snot Is Not the Proper Subject for a Song

Lyrics by Cheryl Miller Thurston
Music by Heather Stenner

It may not be a proper subject, but it's a funny one!

See page 151 for accompaniment.

Warm-Ups and Rounds

Pat Picked Pepperoni Pizza

Lyrics by Cheryl Miller Thurston
Music by Heather Stenner

(continue up by half steps)

See page 154 for accompaniment.

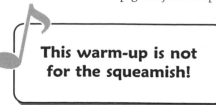

This warm-up is not for the squeamish!

67

Wiggle Your Fingers

Lyrics by Cheryl Miller Thurston
Music by Heather Stenner

Wig-gle your fin - gers. Wig-gle your toes. Wig-gle your eye - balls.

Wig - gle your nose. Wig - gle your el - bows,

read - y or not. Now wig -gle ev -'ry thing you've got.

Wig-gle your fin - gers. Wig-gle your toes. Wig-gle your eye - balls.

Wig - gle your nose. Wig - gle your el - bows,

read - y or not. Now wig -gle ev -'ry thing you've got.

(continue up to the Key of E, then F and then G.)

See page 157 for accompaniment.

Your whole body gets involved with this warm-up.

Never Hug an Alligator

Lyrics by Cheryl Miller Thurston
Music by Heather Stenner

Nev - er hug an al - li - ga - tor. Nev - er kiss a fish. No!

Nev - er hug an al - li - ga - tor. Nev - er kiss a fish. No!

Nev - er hug an al - li - ga - tor. Nev - er kiss a fish, No! *

*Continue up
by half steps*

See page 162 for accompaniment.

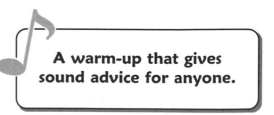

A warm-up that gives sound advice for anyone.

I've Got a Cat

Lyrics by Cheryl Miller Thurston
Music by Heather Stenner

I've got a cat with nine lives. I've got a cat. Splat!

I've got a cat with eight lives. I've got a cat. Splat!

I've got a cat with sev - en lives. I've got a cat. Splat! *

Continue up by half steps.

I've got a cat with six lives. I've got a cat. Splat!
I've got a cat with five lives. I've got a cat. Splat!
(Continue in this manner until the last verse)

I've got a cat with one life. That's e-nough for her. Purr!

rit.

See page 164 for accompaniment.

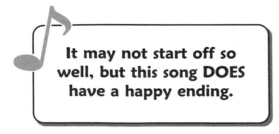

It may not start off so well, but this song DOES have a happy ending.

Ecka Booly

Lyrics by Cheryl Miller Thurston
Music by Heather Stenner

Continue up by half steps

See page 166 for accompaniment.

If you sing it fast enough, will you sound a bit precocious? See how fast you can go before your tongue becomes tangled.

Macaroni and Cheese

Lyrics by Cheryl Miller Thurston
Music by Heather Stenner

In a whining manner

Mac - a - ron - i and cheese.___ Mac - a - ron - i and cheese.___

Oh, won't you please___ give me mac and cheese.___ Oh, won't you

please___ give me mac and cheese? I don't want

mashed po - ta - toes or peas.___ I've got a mac and cheese___ dis -

ease. So won't you please___ give me mac and cheese?

See page 167 for accompaniment.

This warm-up encourages you to be as dramatic as possible. Really WHINE on this one.

Itsy Bitsy Down the Drain

Lyrics by Cheryl Miller Thurston
Music by Heather Stenner

A sad tale, in a chromatic scale.

See page 169 for accompaniment.

Boom Snap Clap

Lyrics by Cheryl Miller Thurston
Music by Heather Stenner

Boom snap clap boom boom snap clap snap. Boom snap clap boom boom snap clap snap

boom. Two! Three! Warm it up! Boom snap clap boom boom snap clap snap.

Boom snap clap boom boom snap clap snap boom. Two! Three! Give it more now!

See page 172 for accompaniment.

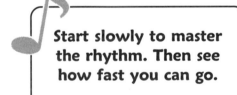

Start slowly to master the rhythm. Then see how fast you can go.

With the word "boom," hit one hand on your chest.
With "snap," snap your fingers.
With "clap," clap your hands.
For a real challenge, do the actions without saying the words.

For more "Warm-Ups and Rounds," see also:

Victor Vacuumed, page 34
Never Hug a Hibble, page 49
M & Ms, page 88

Songs for More than One Person

Tuna Fish Ice Cream

Lyrics by Cheryl Miller Thurston
Music by Heather Stenner

Two part

See page 173 for accompaniment.

This two-part song could make you lose your appetite....

Picking Up a Pepperoni Pizza

Lyrics by Cheryl Miller Thurston
Arr. by Heather Stenner

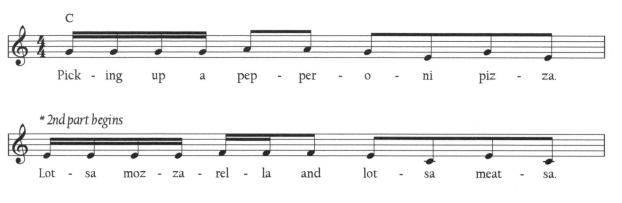

Pick - ing up a pep - per - o - ni piz - za.

2nd part begins

Lot - sa moz - za - rel - la and lot - sa meat - sa.

3rd part begins

I love a piz - za pie! Big - a bite - a piz - za, me oh my!

See page 174 for accompaniment.

A three-part round with an Italian flavor, set to the tune of an Australian folk song, "Kookaburra."

My Name Is

Lyrics by Cheryl Miller Thurston
Music by Heather Stenner

(In a very "proper" or haughty manner, if possible, for the girls)

Girls: My name is Sar - ah Sa - man - tha Su - san Ce - cil - ia Em - ma - bem - ma Bil - lings - ley Har - ring - ton Hobb. That's my name, and here's my friend, and he'll tell you his name:

Boys. Bob.

* *Increase the tempo with each repetition.*

See page 175 for accompaniment.

The boys get only one line, but it's a good one! Repeat the song faster and faster each time.

Doo-Be-Dop

Lyrics by Cheryl Miller Thurston
Music by Heather Stenner

SINGuini • Copyright © 2006 by Cottonwood Press, Inc. • www.cottonwoodpress.com • All rights reserved.

PART III *(Begin 3rd time through)*

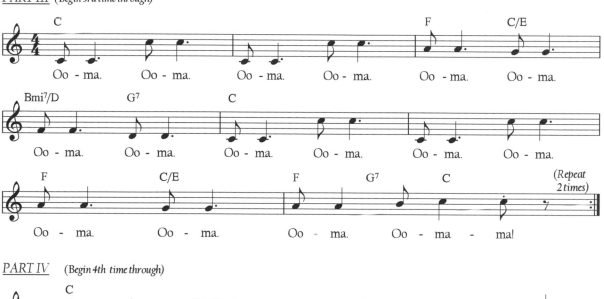

Oo - ma. Oo - ma. Oo - ma. Oo - ma. Oo - ma. Oo - ma.

Oo - ma. Oo - ma. Oo - ma. Oo - ma. Oo - ma. Oo - ma.

Oo - ma. Oo - ma. Oo - ma. Oo - ma - ma!

(Repeat 2 times)

PART IV *(Begin 4th time through)*

Shu - bah. Shu - bah, shu - bah, shu - bah, shu - bah.

Shu - bah - shu - bah, shu - bah - shu - bah, shu - ba - shu - bah, shu - bah.

Shu - bah. Shu - bah, shu - bah, shu - bah, shu - bah.

Shu - bah - shu - bah, shu - bah - shu - bah, shu - bah - shu - bah, shu - bah. Shu!

(Repeat 1 time)

See page 176 for accompaniment.

Part I sings alone the first time through. Part II joins on the second time through, and so on. A great sound!

Country Band

Lyrics by Cheryl Miller Thurston
Music by Heather Stenner

PART I

I play drums in a coun-try band. I play drums when - ev-er I can._____

(Repeat 4 times)

Wham! Bam! Whomp-i-ty bomp. Wham! Bam! Whomp-i-ty, whomp-i-ty bomp!

PART II (Begin 2nd time through)

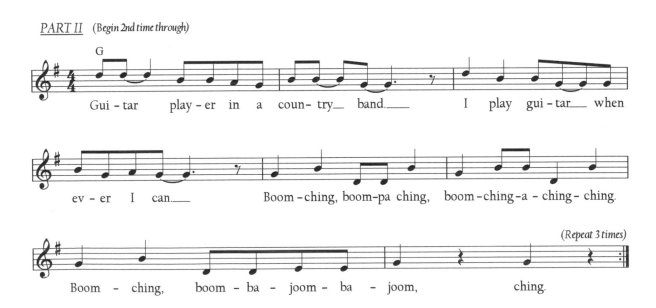

Gui-tar play-er in a coun-try_ band._ I play gui-tar_ when

ev - er I can.__ Boom-ching, boom-pa ching, boom-ching-a - ching-ching.

(Repeat 3 times)

Boom - ching, boom - ba - joom - ba - joom, ching.

PART III (Begin 3rd time through)

G

I fid - dle with my fid - dle. I fid - dle with my fid - dle. I

fid - dle with my fid - dle when - ev - ver I can.___ I

fid - dle with my fid - dle. I fid - dle with my fid - dle. I

(Repeat 2 times)

fid - dle with my fid - dle when - ev - er I can.___

PART IV (Begin 4th time through)

G

I'm the sing-er for a coun-try band. I sing songs when-ev-er I can. Like,

(Repeat 1 time)

"My true love left me feel-in'___ blue. He took my heart and my pick-up___ too."
(She)

See page 178 for accompaniment.

♪ **Sing this song with a country twang. Part I sings alone the first time through. Part II joins on the second time through, and so on.**

83

I Love My Neck

Lyrics by Cheryl Miller Thurston
Music by Heather Stenner

See page 180 for accompaniment.

A song about a body part we usually take for granted.

Emma Wants Ice Cream

Lyrics by Cheryl Miller Thurston
Music by Heather Stenner

(* Leader points to someone who becomes the new leader.)

See page 182 for accompaniment.

Whoever is leader chooses what Emma wants. You can substitute different names for "Emma," too.

Good Night and Monsters in My Closet

Lyrics by Cheryl Miller Thurston
Music by Heather Stenner

Good Night

Good night. Sleep tight. Don't let the
bed-bugs bite. Good night. Sleep tight. But if they do bite,
bite them back and they won't be back to-mor-row night.

Monsters in My Closet

Mon-sters in my clos-et. Mon-sters un-der my
bed._____ Want to get those mon-sters and
bash 'em in the head._____ Then I'll get some sleep!

See page 185 for accompaniment.

What is a partner song? Two songs that are sung at the same time and fit together perfectly.

Dancing on a Daisy and Goop Glop

Lyrics by Cheryl Miller Thurston
Music by Heather Stenner

Dancing on a Daisy

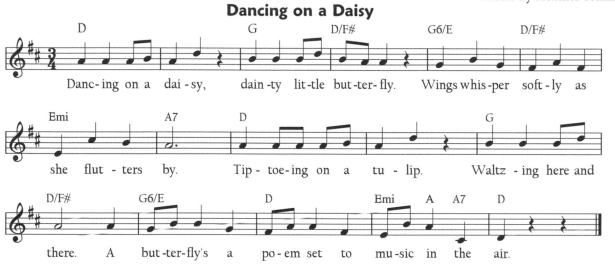

Danc-ing on a dai-sy, dain-ty lit-tle but-ter-fly. Wings whis-per soft-ly as she flut-ters by. Tip-toe-ing on a tu-lip. Waltz-ing here and there. A but-ter-fly's a po-em set to mu-sic in the air.

Goop Glop

Goop! Glop! Sludge! Slop! Mud-dy pud-dles of grue-some gunk. Sleaze! Slime! Grease! Grime! (spoken) Ewwww! Aw-ful a-ro-ma of skunk.

See page 187 for accompaniment.

Another partner song.

M & Ms

Lyrics by Cheryl Miller Thurston
Music by Heather Stenner

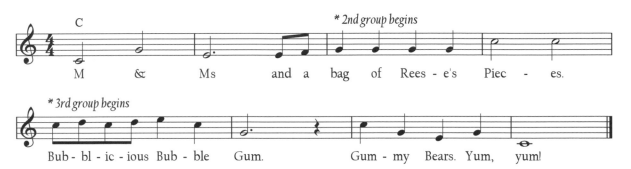

A three-part round that will make you hungry.

See page 189 for accompaniment.

ACCOMPANIMENT

Bill Loves Jill

Lyrics by Cheryl Miller Thurston
Arr. by Heather Stenner

Ann loves Dan.
Ann loves Dan.
Dan loves Dee.
Dan loves Dee.

But Dee's beloved is Anthony,
and his beloved is Bethany,
and her beloved is Timothy,
But he loves Ann.

My Bonnie Went in for a Face Lift

Lyrics by Cheryl Miller Thurston
Arr. by Heather Stenner

Z-Y-X

Lyrics by Cheryl Miller Thurston
Arr. by Heather Stenner

Oh, My Darling Frankensteen

Lyrics by Cheryl Miller Thurston
Arr. by Heather Stenner

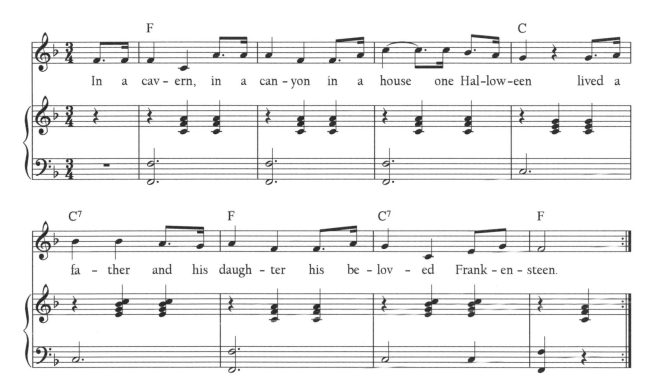

In a cav-ern, in a can-yon in a house one Hal-low-een lived a fa-ther and his daugh-ter his be-lov-ed Frank-en-steen.

He had built her in his lab
with a bizarre and big machine.
And he loved her very dearly,
his beloved Frankensteen.

She was not a natural beauty.
She wore shoes, size seventeen.
All her hair was made of barbed wire,
and her face was olive green.

Both her eyes were bolted on with
lots of chicken wire between.
What had once been part of fencing
was a nose on Frankensteen.

He decided she should marry,
but the men around were mean.
Not a one would even talk to
his beloved Frankensteen.

So he went into his lab
to his bizarre and big machine,
and he built a future husband
for his darling Frankensteen.

Plugged him in and called his daughter
and said, "Darling, meet Eugene."
And she sighed to see the cutest
guy she'd ever, ever seen.

It was instant love for both, and
sparks were flying at the scene.
But alas, there was some gas, and
they were blown to smithereens.

Oh, his darling, oh, his darling,
Oh, his darling Frankensteen.
She is lost and gone forever,
but at least she's with Eugene.

95

On Top of a Bald Guy

Lyrics by Cheryl Miller Thurston
Arr. by Heather Stenner

For additional verses, see "Melody Only" section, page 17,
or "Lyrics at a Glance," page 194

My Bike Has a Flat Tire

Lyrics by Cheryl Miller Thurston
Arr. by Heather Stenner

For additional verses, see "Melody Only" section, page 19,
or "Lyrics at a Glance," page 194

Mary Possessed a Petite
Offspring of a Ewe

Lyrics by Cheryl Miller Thurston
Arr. by Heather Stenner

For additional verses, see "Melody Only" section, page 20,
or "Lyrics at a Glance," page 195

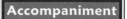

A Spaceship Landed

Lyrics by Cheryl Miller Thurston
Arr. by Heather Stenner

(continued)

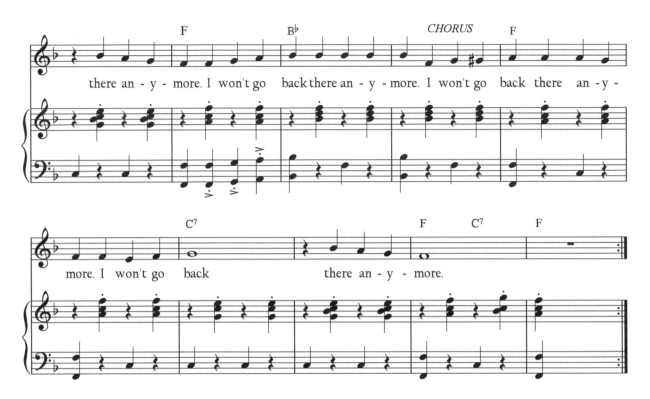

For additional verses, see "Melody Only" section, page 23,
or "Lyrics at a Glance," page 195

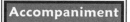

I Am the Very Model of a Perfect Son or Daughter

Lyrics by Cheryl Miller Thurston
Arr. by Heather Stenner

(continued)

do the dish - es cheer - ful - ly and e - ven put them all a - way, and

when it's eight p. m., I know it's time for me to hit the hay. I'm

al - ways so po - lite. I say, "Ex - cuse me, sir," and "Par - don me." I'm

(continued)

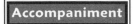

There's a House in the Middle of the Town

Lyrics by Cheryl Miller Thurston
Arr. by Heather Stenner

(continued)

For additional verses, see "Melody Only" section, page 27,
or "Lyrics at a Glance," page 196

SINGuini ● Copyright © 2006 by Cottonwood Press, Inc. ● www.cottonwoodpress.com ● All rights reserved.

Boa Constrictor

Lyrics by Cheryl Miller Thurston
Music by Heather Stenner

(continued)

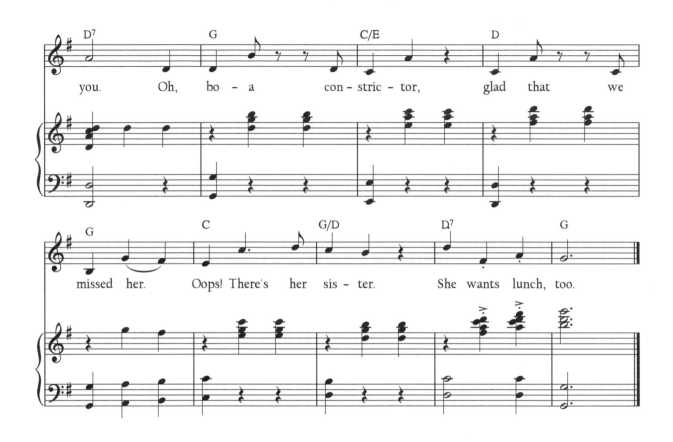

Whiffling, Waffling Will

Lyrics by Cheryl Miller Thurston
Music by Heather Stenner

(continued)

Victor Vacuumed

Lyrics by Cheryl Miller Thurston
Music by Heather Stenner

(continued)

Peas

Lyrics by Cheryl Miller Thurston
Music by Heather Stenner

SINGuini • Copyright © 2006 by Cottonwood Press, Inc. • www.cottonwoodpress.com • All rights reserved.

no," I said, 'Thank you, sir. I think soup's what I pre - fer. Make it
no," I said, 'Bring me cheese with my SOUP, sir, if you please. Oh,—

beef noo - dle, if you please." He said, 'What I'll give you, sir, is
no," I said. 'Bring me cheese." He said, 'What I'll give you, sir, is

peas and peas and peas and peas and peas. Just peas!"
peas and peas and peas and peas and peas. Just peas!"

For additional verses, see "Melody Only" section, page 37,
or "Lyrics at a Glance," page 198

Alexander's Outside Eating Bugs

Lyrics by Cheryl Miller Thurston
Arr. by Heather Stenner

Al - ex - an - der's out - side eat - ing bugs. Al - ex - an - der's kind of weak on

hy - giene. If I make him stop, then he will cry a lot and

scream! *(Screamed: EE EEEE EEEEE EEEEEE EEEEEEE!)* Al - ex - an - der's eat - ing lit - tle

(continued)

Cell Phone Song

Lyrics by Cheryl Miller Thurston
Arr. by Heather Stenner

SINGuini • Copyright © 2006 by Cottonwood Press, Inc. • www.cottonwoodpress.com • All rights reserved.

We got so mad. A man be-gan to talk a-bout his gro - c'ries. They need-ed bread. They need-ed bread. And, yes, he'd get some milk and may-be

(continued)

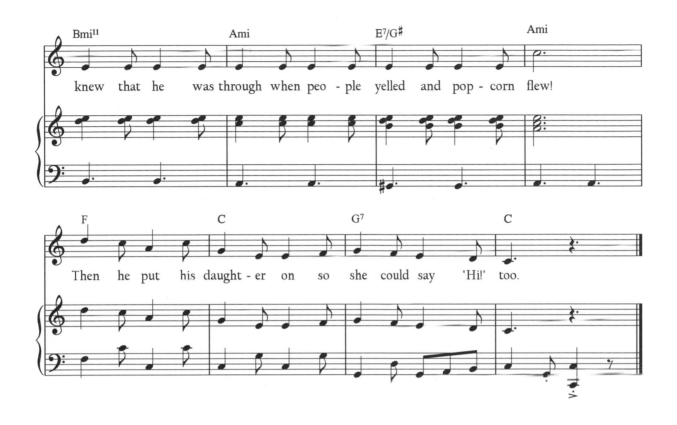

Don't Wanna Be a Couch Potato

Lyrics by Cheryl Miller Thurston
Music by Heather Stenner

(continued)

D.C. al Coda

through his___ house, that fel - la did - n't ev - en look up!

CODA

me. It's de - test - a - ble to be a

veg - 'ta - ble. Not me.

rit.

Bill Bought a Backpack Bigger than Bill

Lyrics by Cheryl Miller Thurston
Music by Heather Stenner

CHORUS

Bill bought a back-pack big-ger than Bill.___ Bill bought a back-pack big-ger than Bill.___

Bill bought a back-pack big-ger than Bill.___ Poor, poor, poor___ Bill. Well, he

Verse 1

filled that back-pack and put it___ on. Fell right back-wards on-to the lawn.

For additional verses, see "Melody Only" section, page 45,
or "Lyrics at a Glance," page 199

Never Hug a Hibble

Lyrics by Cheryl Miller Thurston
Music by Heather Stenner

For additional verses, see "Melody Only" section, page 49,
or "Lyrics at a Glance," page 199

Her Poodle Likes Noodles

Lyrics by Cheryl Miller Thurston
Music by Heather Stenner

(continued)

all day long, and some-times her box-er likes shorts._____ Her

schnau-zer likes trou-sers. Her aire-dale likes planes, and her

grey-hound likes bus-es, of course!

I Like Your Singin'

Lyrics by Cheryl Miller Thurston
Music by Heather Stenner

(continued)

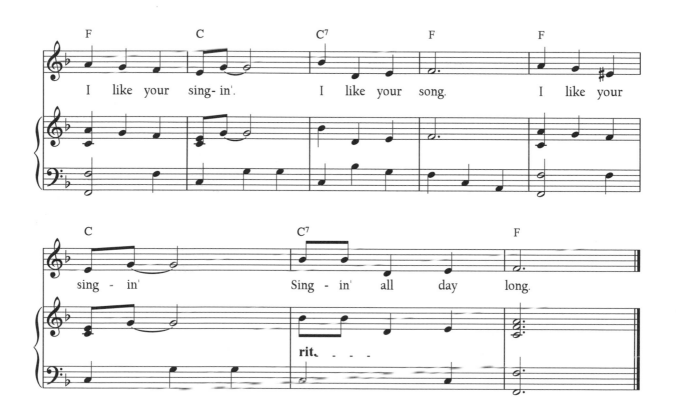

Surfing Polka Band

Lyrics by Cheryl Miller Thurston
Music by Heather Stenner

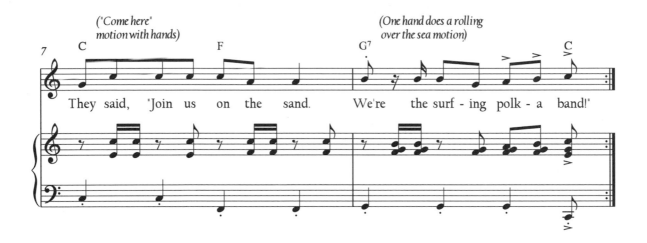

They said, "Join us on the sand. We're the surf-ing polk-a band!"

Impossible to Sing Song

Lyrics by Cheryl Miller Thurston
Music by Heather Stenner

   SINGuini • Copyright © 2006 by Cottonwood Press, Inc. • www.cottonwoodpress.com •

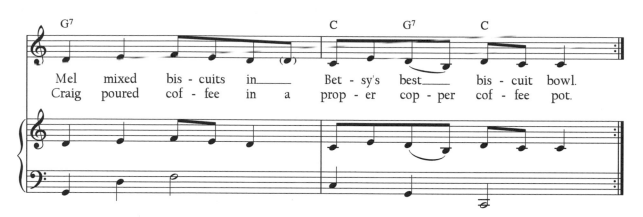

Mel mixed bis - cuits in Bet - sy's best bis - cuit bowl.
Craig poured cof - fee in a prop - er cop - per cof - fee pot.

For additional verses, see "Melody Only" section, page 57, or "Lyrics at a Glance," page 200

Ugh!

Lyrics by Cheryl Miller Thurston
Music by Heather Stenner

Motions

On "pat," alternate between patting your left and right leg.
On "clap," clap your hands together.

During this section, keep a stomping beat in your feet.

"ugh" is an ug - ug - ug - ug - ly word. Oh, "ugh" is an ug - ly - word. (clap, clap) Oh,

(continued)

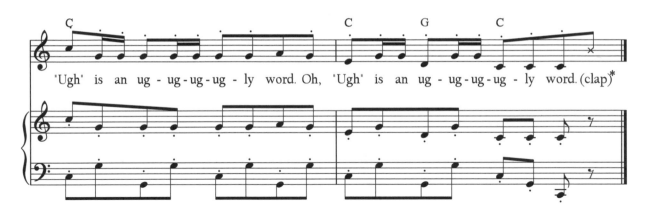

"Ugh" is an ug - ug - ug - ug - ly word. Oh, "Ugh" is an ug - ug - ug - ug - ly word. (clap)

* Repeat from beginning again and again until exhausted!

This Is a Boring Song

Lyrics by Cheryl Miller Thurston
Music by Heather Stenner

(continued)

That's the kind of de-tail that a per-son needs to men-tion, if a song like this is ev-er going to get an-y-one's un-di-vid-ed at-ten-tion.

Yes!

Lyrics by Cheryl Miller Thurston
Arr. by Heather Stenner

(continued)

Snot Is Not the Proper Subject for a Song

Lyrics by Cheryl Miller Thurston
Music by Heather Stenner

(continued)

Pat Picked Pepperoni Pizza

Lyrics by Cheryl Miller Thurston
Music by Heather Stenner

SINGuini • Copyright © 2006 by Cottonwood Press, Inc. • www.cottonwoodpress.com • All rights reserved.

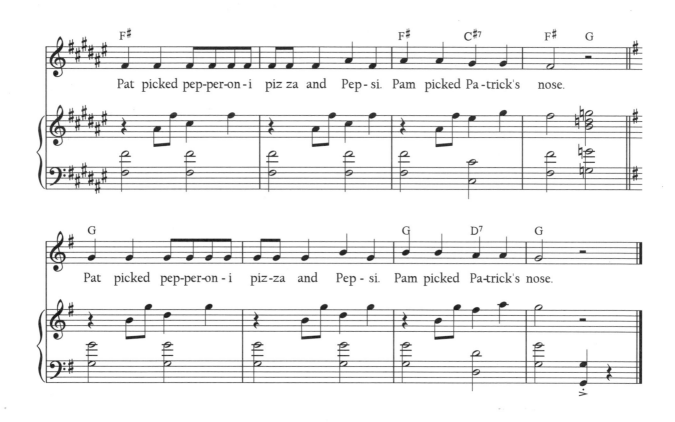

Wiggle Your Fingers

Lyrics by Cheryl Miller Thurston
Music by Heather Stenner

(continued)

159

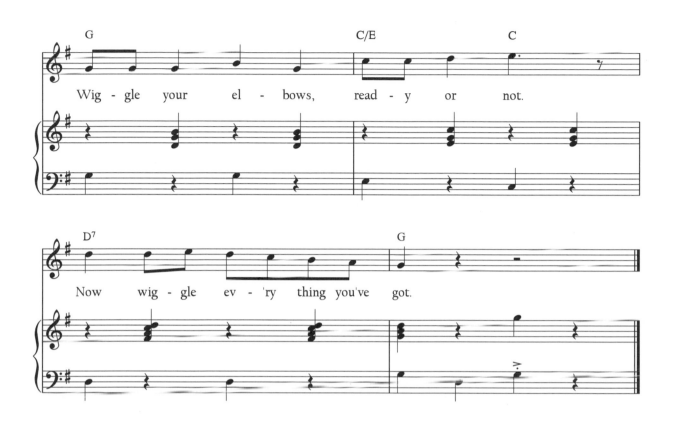

Never Hug an Alligator

Lyrics by Cheryl Miller Thurston
Music by Heather Stenner

I've Got a Cat

Lyrics by Cheryl Miller Thurston
Music by Heather Stenner

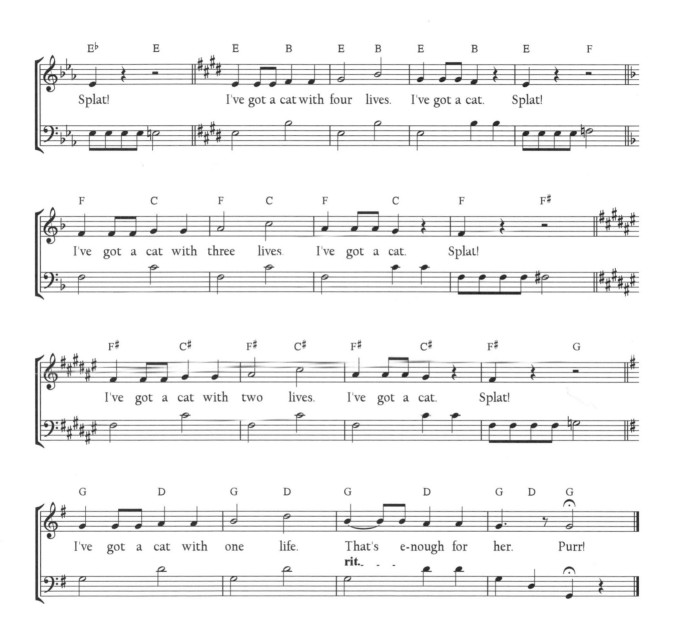

Ecka Booly

Lyrics by Cheryl Miller Thurston
Music by Heather Stenner

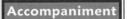

Macaroni and Cheese

Lyrics by Cheryl Miller Thurston
Music by Heather Stenner

(continued)

Itsy Bitsy Down the Drain

Lyrics by Cheryl Miller Thurston
Music by Heather Stenner

(continued)

Boom Snap Clap

Lyrics by Cheryl Miller Thurston
Music by Heather Stenner

*Repeat the three measure
pattern over and over.*

With the word "boom," hit one hand on your chest.
With "snap," snap your fingers.
With "clap," clap your hands.
For a real challenge, do the actions without saying the words.

Tuna Fish Ice Cream

Lyrics by Cheryl Miller Thurston
Music by Heather Stenner

Tu-na fish   ice cream,   cau-li-flow-er cup-cakes,   cook-ies with on-ions   and choc'-late chips!

Two part

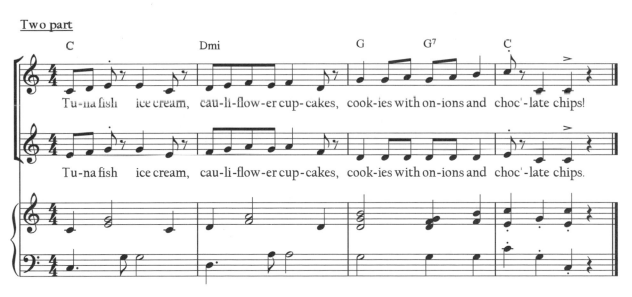

Tu-na fish   ice cream,   cau-li-flow-er cup-cakes,   cook-ies with on-ions and   choc'-late chips!

Tu-na fish   ice cream,   cau-li-flow-er cup-cakes,   cook-ies with on-ions and   choc'-late chips.

Picking Up a Pepperoni Pizza

Lyrics by Cheryl Miller Thurston
Arr. by Heather Stenner

My Name Is

Lyrics by Cheryl Miller Thurston
Music by Heather Stenner

(In a very "proper" or haughty manner, if possible, for the girls)

Girls: My name is Sar-ah Sa-man-tha Su-san Ce-cil-ia Em-ma-bem-ma Bil-lings-ley Har-ring-ton Hobb. That's my name, and here's my friend, and he'll tell you his name:

Boys: Bob.

* *Increase the tempo with each repetition.*

Doo-Be-Dop

Lyrics by Cheryl Miller Thurston
Music by Heather Stenner

Country Band

Lyrics by Cheryl Miller Thurston
Music by Heather Stenner

179

I Love My Neck

Lyrics by Cheryl Miller Thurston
Music by Heather Stenner

be, should be! spine, my spine! My neck is fan-tas-tic. It high-lights my

chin, and it al-ways looks per-fect to me, to me. It's al-so so

hand-y for hold-ing my head up so it won't fall on-to my knee, my knee. Oh,

Emma Wants Ice Cream

Lyrics by Cheryl Miller Thurston
Music by Heather Stenner

(* Leader points to someone who becomes the new leader.)

(continued)

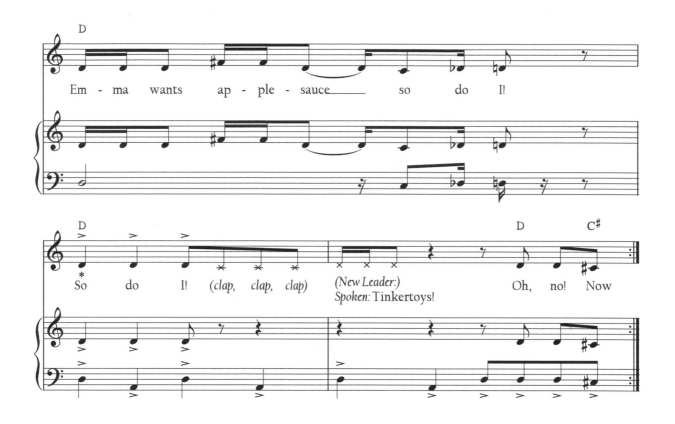

A Suggestion for music teachers:
Try singing this song in the key of F to work the break
between your student's head and chest voice.

Good Night and Monsters in My Closet

Lyrics by Cheryl Miller Thurston
Music by Heather Stenner

(continued)

Dancing on a Daisy and Goop Glop

Lyrics by Cheryl Miller Thurston
Music by Heather Stenner

(continued)

M & Ms

Lyrics by Cheryl Miller Thurston
Music by Heather Stenner

LYRICS
AT A GLANCE

Bill Loves Jill (13, 91)

Bill loves Jill.
Bill loves Jill.
Jill loves Joe.
Jill loves Joe.
But Joe's beloved is Annalee,
And her beloved is Jeremy,
And his beloved is Brittany,
But she loves Bill!

Ann loves Dan.
Ann loves Dan.
Dan loves Dee.
Dan loves Dee.
But Dee's beloved is Anthony,
and his beloved is Bethany,
and her beloved is Timothy,
But he loves Ann!

My Bonnie Went in for a Face Lift (14, 92)

My Bonnie went in for a face lift.
My Bonnie received a new nose.
My Bonnie lost all of her wrinkles.
She's now someone nobody knows.

Bring back, bring back,
Oh, bring back my Bonnie to me, to me.
Bring back, bring back,
Oh, bring back my Bonnie to me.

My Bonnie lost all of her chins, and
The pouches below both her eyes.
Her skin is now smooth as a baby's—
She's nobody I recognize.

Bring back, bring back,
Oh, bring back my Bonnie to me, to me.
Bring back, bring back,
Oh, bring back my Bonnie to me.

Z-Y-X (15, 94)

ZYX, double-u, VUT,
S and R and Q and P,
ONML, K and J,
IHGFEDCBA.
Now I've sung it all the way,
The alphabet backwards, Z to A!

Oh, My Darling Frankensteen (16, 95)

In a cavern, in a canyon,
in a house one Halloween
lived a father and his daughter,
his beloved Frankensteen.

He had built her in his lab with
a bizarre and big machine.
And he loved her very dearly,
his beloved Frankensteen.

She was not a natural beauty.
She wore shoes, size seventeen.
All her hair was made of barbed wire,
and her face was olive green.

Both her eyes were bolted on with
lots of chicken wire between.
What had once been part of fencing
was a nose on Frankensteen.

He decided she should marry,
but the men around were mean.
Not a one would even talk to
his beloved Frankensteen.

So he went into his lab to
his bizarre and big machine,
and he built a future husband
for his darling Frankensteen.

Plugged him in and called his daughter
and said, "Darling, meet Eugene."
And she sighed to see the cutest
guy she'd ever, ever seen.

It was instant love for both, and
sparks were flying at the scene.
But alas, there was some gas, and
they were blown to smithereens.

Oh, his darling, oh his darling,
Oh, his darling, Frankensteen.
She is lost and gone forever,
but at least she's with Eugene.

On Top of a Bald Guy (17, 96)

On top of a bald guy,
Asleep on the sand,
my sister drew pictures
while he simply tanned.

She used Magic Markers,
in purple and red.
She drew little flowers
all over his head.

She added a mustache
right under his nose,
and there on his forehead,
she painted a rose.

And when he turned over
and started to snore,
she added some tulips
and daisies and more.

But when the guy snorted
and started to wake,
my sister decided,
"Hey, time for a break."

She went in the ocean.
I stayed in my chair
to watch the old bald guy
with flowers for hair.

I couldn't help laughing.
He looked so confused.
He wondered why others
were looking amused.

He borrowed a mirror
and saw his new hair.
He saw all the flowers
and me sitting there.

He jumped to conclusions.
He started to growl.
I jumped to my feet as
he jumped from his towel.

I ran to the ocean.
He ran after me.
My sister just smiled as
I jumped in the sea.

I'm still treading water.
My future is grim.
But I sure am happy
That bald guy can't swim!

My Bike Has a Flat Tire (18, 97)

Nathaniel:
My bike has a flat tire, Amanda, Amanda.
My bike has a flat tire, Amanda, a flat.

Amanda:
Then fix it, Nathaniel, Nathaniel, Nathaniel.
Then fix it, Nathaniel, Nathaniel, fix it.

Nathaniel:
But how should I fix it, Amanda, Amanda?
But how should I fix it, Amanda, but how?

Amanda:
With a bike pump, Nathaniel, Nathaniel, Nathaniel.
With a bike pump, Nathaniel, Nathaniel, a pump.

Nathaniel:
But the pump handle's broken, Amanda, Amanda.
But the pump handle's broken. Amanda, it's broke.

Amanda:
Then glue it, Nathaniel, Nathaniel, Nathaniel.
Then glue it, Nathaniel, Nathaniel, glue it.

Nathaniel:
I'm all out of glue, Amanda, Amanda.
I'm all out of glue, Amanda, no glue.

Amanda:
Then buy some, Nathaniel, Nathaniel, Nathaniel.
Then buy some, Nathaniel, Nathaniel, buy some.

Nathaniel:
But where should I buy it, Amanda, Amanda?
But where should I buy it, Amanda, but where?

Amanda:
At WalMart, Nathaniel, Nathaniel, Nathaniel.
At WalMart, Nathaniel, Nathaniel, WalMart.

Nathaniel:
But how should I get there, Amanda, Amanda?
But how should I get there, Amanda, but how?

Amanda:
On your bi-ike, Nathaniel, Nathaniel, Nathaniel.
On your bi-ike, Nathaniel, Nathaniel, your bike.

Nathaniel:
My bike has a flat tire, Amanda, Amanda!
My bike has a flat tire, Amanda, a flat!!!!!

Mary Possessed a Petite Offspring of a Ewe (20, 98)

Mary possessed a petite offspring of a ewe,
Offspring of a ewe, offspring of a ewe.
Mary possessed a petite offspring of a ewe.
Its coat of wool was as white as precipitation from the
    sky in winter.

It proceeded after her to an institution of learning one day,
Learning one day, learning one day.
It proceeded after her to an institution of learning one day,
which violated all the regulations imposed by the
    authorities.

It caused the students to show amusement and frolic and
    cavort,
Frolic and cavort, frolic and cavort.
It caused the students to show amusement and frolic and
    cavort,
to observe the offspring of a ewe at an institution of
    learning.

A Spaceship Landed (22, 99)

Oh, a spaceship landed (Oh, a spaceship landed)
in my back yard. (In my back yard.)
It came in fast. (It came in fast)
It landed hard. (It landed hard.)
Oh, a spaceship landed in my back yard.
It came in fast and landed hard.
I won't go back there anymore.

Chorus
I won't go back there anymore.
I won't go back there anymore
I won't go back there anymore.

(continue echoing first four lines, as above)

Oh, the top popped open.
They all came out.
They had green ears
and purple snouts.
Oh, the top popped open. They all came out.
They had green ears and purple snouts.
I won't go back there anymore.

Chorus

Oh, they waved their arms.
They had sixteen.
They looked dressed up
for Halloween.
They waved their arms. They had sixteen.
They looked dressed up for Halloween.
I won't go back there anymore.

Chorus

Oh, they held up signs
that made no sense.
They opened packs
and pitched some tents.
They held up signs that made no sense.
They opened packs and pitched some tents.
I won't go back there anymore.

Chorus

Oh, it's been a year.
They haven't left.
They ate my lawn.
There's nothing left.
It's been a year. They haven't left.
They ate my lawn. There's nothing left.
I won't go back there anymore.

Chorus

Oh, they sing all night.
They never miss.
They sing a song
that goes like this:
Ziddle-op-dorp-giddle-op, ziddle-iddle-ay.
Ziddle-op-dorp-giddle-op, ziddle-iddle-ay.
Ziddle-op-dorp-dorp, ziddle-iddle-iddle-ay.

195

I Am the Very Model of a Perfect Son or Daughter (24, 101)

I am the very model of a perfect son or daughter
'cause I always do the things my mother tells me that I
oughter,
like I always hang my clothes up, and I fold my laundry
carefully.
I never leave the milk out on the counter accidentally.

My fav'rite snack is cel'ry and I think it tastes sensational.
I never watch a TV show unless it's educational.
I do the dishes cheerfully and even put them all away,
and when it's eight p. m., I know it's time for me to hit the
hay.

I'm always so polite. I say, "Excuse me, sir," and "Pardon
me."
I'm never late or find myself somewhere I'm not supposed
to be.
I never make mistakes, you see. I live my life so carefully,
and maybe that is why nobody wants to spend much time
with me.

There's a House in the Middle of the Town (26, 105)

There's a house in the middle of the town.
There's a house in the middle of the town.
There's a house. There's a house.
There's a house in the middle of the town.

There's a chair in the house in the middle of the town.
There's a chair in the house in the middle of the town.
There's a chair. There's a chair.
There's a chair in the house in the middle of the town.

There's a child in the chair in the house in the middle of
the town.
There's a child in the chair in the house in the middle of
the town.
There's a child. There's a child.
There's a child in the chair in the house in the middle of
the town.

There's a bib on the child in the chair in the house in the
middle of the town.
There's a bib on the child in the chair in the house in the
middle of the town.
There's a bib. There's a bib.
There's a bib on the child in the chair in the house in the
middle of the town.

There's a drip on the bib on the child in the chair in the
house in the middle of the town.
There's a drip on the bib on the child in the chair in the
house in the middle of the town.
There's a drip. There's a drip.
There's a drip on the bib on the child in the chair in the
house in the middle of the town.

There's a fly on the drip on the bib on the child in the
chair in the house in the middle of the town.
There's a fly on the drip on the bib on the child in the
chair in the house in the middle of the town.
There's a fly. There's a fly.
There's a fly on the drip on the bib on the child in the
chair in the house in the middle of the town.

There's a flea on the fly on the drip on the bib on the child
in the chair in the house in the middle of the town.
There's a flea on the fly on the drip on the bib on the child
in the chair in the house in the middle of the town.
There's a flea. There's a flea.
There's a flea on the fly on the drip on the bib on the child
in the chair in the house in the middle of the town.

There's a speck on the flea on the fly on the drip on the
bib on the child in the chair in the house in the middle
of the town.
There's a speck on the flea on the fly on the drip on the
bib on the child in the chair in the house in the middle
of the town.
There's a speck. There's a speck.
There's a speck on the flea on the fly on the drip on the
bib on the child in the chair in the house in the middle
of the town.

Boa Constrictor (31, 107)

Boa constrictor
already picked her
lunch, and it's Mister
Boggs and his dog.

Oh, she likes to squeeze.
She won't take time to chew.
She swallows things whole,
better hope it's not you.

Oh, boa constrictor,
glad that we missed her.
Oops! There's her sister.
She wants lunch, too!

Whiffling Waffling Will (32, 109)

Oh, my boyfriend Will wouldn't make up his mind.
He said, "Yes, maybe no, maybe yes, maybe no."
He whiffled and waffled most all of the time,
and his hemming and hawing was way out of line.

Chorus
Whiffling, waffling, whiffling Will.
Whiffling, waffling, whiffling Will.
Whiffling, waffling, whiffling Will.
Whiffling, waffling, whiffling Will.

I asked my boyfriend to go to the show.
He said, "Yes, maybe no, maybe yes, maybe no."
He couldn't decide if he wanted to go,
so he said, "Flip a coin 'cause I really don't know."

Chorus

I asked my boyfriend to go for a ride.
He said, "Yes, maybe no, maybe yes, maybe no."
I got out my bike, but he couldn't decide,
so I said, "I have had it, and this is 'Goodbye'."

Chorus

Victor Vacuumed (34, 111)

Victor vacuumed up a beetle, crawling by his chair.
Though the beetle wasn't happy, Victor didn't care.

Victor vacuumed up a spider, spinning by his chair.
Though the spider wasn't happy, Victor didn't care.

Victor vacuumed up his kitten, purring on his chair.
Though the kitten wasn't happy, Victor didn't care.

Victor vacuumed up his puppy, resting on his chair.
Though the puppy wasn't happy, Victor didn't care.

Victor vacuumed up his sister, crawling by his chair.
Though his sister wasn't happy, Victor didn't care.

Victor's sister crawled back out and stood on Victor's chair.
Then she vacuumed Victor up, and NOW Victor cares!

Peas (36, 114)

Went to a restaurant with my friend.
I asked the waiter what he would recommend.
He said, "The thing you should have is these."
He pointed to a picture of a bowl of peas.

"Oh, no", I said, "Thank you, sir.
I think soup's what I prefer.
Make it beef noodle, if you please."
He said, "What I'll give you, sir, is peas and peas
and peas and peas and peas. Just peas!"

I said, "I think you misunderstood.
I'd never order peas, even if I should."
He said, "The thing you should have is these."
He pointed to a picture of a bowl of peas.

"Oh, no", I said, "Bring me cheese
with my SOUP, sir, if you please.
Oh, no," I said, "Bring me cheese."
He said, "What I'll give you, sir, is peas and peas
and peas and peas and peas. Just peas!"

"I'd like to order now," said my friend.
"I won't be asking what you will recommend.
I think that I will have some of these."
He pointed to the picture of a bowl of peas.

"Oh, no, sir, if you please,
I have promised all our peas.
Oh, no, sir, now it seems
all that I can give you, sir, is beans and beans
and beans and beans and beans. Just beans!"

Alexander's Outside Eating Bugs (38, 116)

Alexander's outside eating bugs.
Alexander's appetite is man-size.
Though he's only three,
he eats enough for me
and doesn't even care if it is dead or it's alive!

Alexander's outside eating bugs.
Alexander's kind of weak on hygiene.
If I make him stop,
then he will cry a lot
and scream!

Alexander's eating little mealybugs and bumblebees
and pickleworms and silverfish
and dragonflies and doggie fleas.
He's swallowing a weevil and a maggot and a millipede,
a termite and a beetle and a cricket and a centipede,
and now he's got a spittlebug,
and now he's got a baby slug!

Alexander's outside eating bugs.
I am inside feeling kind of yucky.
And I wonder, "Must he
be so darned disgusting?" Eeeew! (Spoken: Argh. Ahh.
Urp. Ugh. etc.)
I'm sick!

Cell Phone Song (40, 120)

One day, a friend and I went to a movie,
and it was sad, and it was sad.
But when a cell phone somewhere started ringing,
we got so mad. We got so mad.

A man began to talk about his groc'ries.
They needed bread. They needed bread.
And, yes, he'd get some milk and maybe porkchops,
or beef instead or beef instead.

And, no, he didn't think he'd have
the time to get some gas,
but, yes, when he got home
he would be sure to cut the grass.

We thought we knew that he was through
when people yelled and popcorn flew!
Then he put his daughter on
so she could say "Hi!" too.

Don't Wanna Be a Couch Potato (42, 124)

Don't wanna be a couch potato,
a lump on a sofa or bed.
Don't wanna be a couch potato,
soft as a loafa bread.
I don't wanna be a couch potato.
No, not me!
It's detestable
to be a veg'table.
Not me.

Was a fella watchin' television
all day long.
Was a fella watchin' television.
Didn't matter what was on.
He watched that TV night and day,
couldn't tear himself away.
His muscles turned to mush
and his eyelids wouldn't shut,
and when a six ton truck drove through his house,
that fella didn't even look up!

Don't wanna be a couch potato,
a lump on a sofa or bed.
Don't wanna be a couch potato,
soft as a loafa bread.
I don't wanna be a couch potato.
No, not me!
It's detestable
to be a veg'table.
Not me.
It's detestable to be a veg'table.
Not me.

Bill Bought a Backpack Bigger than Bill (44, 128)

Bill bought a backpack bigger than Bill.
Bill bought a backpack bigger than Bill.
Bill bought a backpack bigger than Bill.
Poor, poor, poor Bill.

Well, he filled that backpack and put it on.
Fell right backwards onto the lawn.
Tried to move but he was stuck.
Poor Bill just couldn't get up.

He tried to move but he was trapped.
He just lay there, on top of his pack.
He hoped someone would happen by
And hear his helpless hopeless cry!

Well, someone finally happened by.
It was his sister Loralei.
She looked at him and then she laughed,
And laughed and laughed and laughed and laughed.

She got her car and got a rope,
Said, "I'll help you, you lit-tle dope."
She tied that rope 'round him where he lay
And one end on the Chevrolet.

Chorus

Well, Loralei said, "Now hold on tight.
I will get you up to-oo-night.
She got in the car and stepped on the gas—
Pulled poor Bill up off his...(pause)...back!

His back, back, back, back, off of his back,
Pulled poor Bi-ill up off of his back.
His back, back, back, back, off of his back.
She saved poor Bill from his pack attack!

Chorus

Never Hug a Hibble (49, 130)

Never hug a hibble in a hibble habble horper.
Never hug a hibble in a hibble habble horp.
Never hug a hibble in a hibble habble horper.
Never hug a hibble at all.

Never bite a bibble in a bibble babble borper.
Never bite a bibble in a bibble babble borp.
Never bite a bibble in a bibble babble borper.
Never bite a bibble at all.

Never squeeze a squibble in a squibble squabble squorper.
Never squeeze a squibble in a squibble squabble squorp.
Never squeeze a squibble in a squibble squabble squorper.
Never squeeze a squibble at all.

Never try a tribble in a tribble trabble trorper.
Never try a tribble in a tribble trabble trorp.
Never try a tribble in a tribble trabble trorper.
Never try a tribble at all.

Her Poodle Likes Noodles (50, 131)

Her poodle likes noodles.
Her pug likes bugs.
Her collie likes polyester.
Her beagle likes bagels.
Her chow likes to chew on the tail of her cat, Sylvester.
Her cockapoo likes lotsa gooey chewy toys.
Her bloodhound likes hounding foxes.
Her Afghan likes oat bran.
Her sheep dog likes sheep,
and her corgi likes corrugated boxes.
Her chow-chow likes bow-wowing all day long,
and sometimes her boxer likes shorts.
Her schnauzer likes trousers.
Her AIRE-dale likes planes,
and her greyhound likes buses, of course!

I Like Your Singin' (52, 134)

Chorus
I like your singin'.
I like your song.
I like your singin'.
Singin' all day long.

Oh, I love to hear you sing,
Boom bop-di-boud.
Don't even care if you
SING IT TOO LOUD!

Chorus

Oh, I love to hear you sing,
"tra-la-la-dee."
Don't even care if you
sing it off-key!

Chorus

Oh, I love to hear you sing,
"flip-flop-di-flong."
Don't even care if your
song is too long.

Chorus

Surfing Polka Band (54, 138)

A man was walking on the beach one day
when he heard an accordion play.
Looked around, saw in the sand
a fiddle in the middle of a polka band.

He said, "May I play with you?
I can yodel-odel-odel-ay-he-hoo. "
They said, "Join us on the sand.
We're the surfing polka band!"

Impossible to Sing Song (56, 140)

Mel mixed biscuits in Betsy's best biscuit bowl.
Mel mixed biscuits in Betsy's best biscuit bowl.
Mel mixed biscuits in Betsy's best biscuit bowl.
Mel mixed biscuits in Betsy's best biscuit bowl.

Craig poured coffee in a proper copper coffee pot.
Craig poured coffee in a proper copper coffee pot.
Craig poured coffee in a proper copper coffee pot.
Craig poured coffee in a proper copper coffee pot.

Sam's sixth sister sizzled thistles in a sausage pan.
Sam's sixth sister sizzled thistles in a sausage pan.
Sam's sixth sister sizzled thistles in a sausage pan.
Sam's sixth sister sizzled thistles in a sausage pan.

Fred fed Ted bread and Ted fed Fred bread.
Fred fed Ted bread and Ted fed Fred bread.
Fred fed Ted bread and Ted fed Fred bread.
Fred fed Ted bread and Ted fed Fred bread.

Mel mixed biscuits in Betsy's best biscuit bowl.
Craig poured coffee in a proper copper coffee pot.
Sam's sixth sister sizzled thistles in a sausage pan.
Fred fed Ted bread and Ted fed Fred bread.

Ugh! (58, 142)

Ugh!
Ugh-a ugh.
Ugh! Ugh!
Ugh-a ugh!
Oh, ugh!
Oh, "ugh" is an ug-ug-ug-ugly word,
Oh, "ugh" is an ugly word.
Oh, "ugh" is an ug-ug-ug-ugly word.
Oh, "ugh" is an ug-ug-ug-ugly word.

This Is a Boring Song (60, 145)

This is a boring song.
The notes are about the same.
This is a boring song.
The words are pretty lame.

This is a boring song.
The words aren't very deep.
This is a boring song.
It's putting me to sleep.

But luckily the chorus really saves this song!
But luckily the chorus has a lot going on.
Like dinosaurs in tutus pirouetting on their toes,
pursued by evil elephants in heels and panty hose.
Hippos doing hip-hop, while a cactus sings the blues.
And crocodiles play poker with a pack of kangaroos.
That's the kind of detail that a person needs to mention,
if a song like this
is ever going to get
anyone's undivided attention.

Yes! (62, 148)

Why not? Why not?
All right, all right, I guess.
I will, I will, I will, I will.
Oh, yes! Yes! Yes!

Okay. Okay.
Uhuh, uhhuh, and yup.
I will, I will, I will, I will, I will,
I will. Thumbs up!

Of course, of course.
Aye-aye, oui, oui, si, si.
Aye-aye, oui, oui.
Aye-aye, oui, oui.
Aye-aye, oui, oui, si, si.

Why not? Why not?
All right, all right, I guess.
I will, I will, I will, I will.
Oh, yes! Yes! Yes!

Okay. Okay.
Uh-uh, uh-huh, and yup.
I will, I will, I will, I will, I will,
I will. Thumbs up!

Snot Is Not the Proper Subject for a Song (64, 151)

Snot is not the proper subject for a song.
Snot is not what you sing about!
Snot is not the proper subject for a song.
Snot!
It's not!

Do not sing about how it is slimy.
Do not sing about how it's not very clean.
Do not sing about how you catch it in a tissue
and look and see it's kind of yellowish green.

Oh, snot is not the proper subject for a song.
Snot is not what you sing about!
Snot is not the proper subject for a song.
Snot!
It's not!

Pat Picked Pepperoni Pizza (67, 154)

Pat picked pepperoni pizza and Pepsi.
Pam picked Patrick's nose.

Wiggle Your Fingers (68, 157)

Wiggle your fingers.
Wiggle your toes.
Wiggle your eyeballs.
Wiggle your nose.
Wiggle your elbows, ready or not.
Now wiggle ev'ry thing you've got.

Never Hug an Alligator (69, 162)

Never hug an alligator.
Never kiss a fish. No! (repeat)

I've Got a Cat (70, 164)

I've got a cat with nine lives.
I've got a cat. Splat!

I've got a cat with eight lives.
I've got a cat. Splat!

I've got a cat with seven lives.
I've got a cat. Splat!

I've got a cat with six lives.
I've got a cat. Splat!

I've got a cat with five lives.
I've got a cat. Splat!

I've got a cat with four lives.
I've got a cat. Splat!

I've got a cat with three lives.
I've got a cat. Splat!

I've got a cat with two lives.
I've got a cat. Splat!

I've got a cat with one life.
That's enough for her. Purr!

Ecka Booly (71, 166)

Ecka booly, cooly ooly,
daba-dooba, mooma-looma.
Splink, splank, splunk.

Macaroni and Cheese (72, 167)

Macaroni and cheese,
Macaroni and cheese,
Oh, won't you please,
give me mac and cheese?
Oh, won't you please,
give me mac and cheese?
I don't want mashed potatoes or peas.
I've got a mac and cheese disease.
So won't you please
give me mac and cheese?

Itsy Bitsy Down the Drain (73, 169)

Itsy Bitsy Spider climbed right up the water spout.
But someone turned the water on and washed that spider
    out.
Oh, Itsy Bitsy Spider frowned and said, "Oh, what a pain!"
But that was right before the water washed him down the
    drain.
Oh, Itsy Bitsy Spider lives in spider heaven now,
where faucets don't have water and a spider never drowns.
Now if you think my story's gruesome, I could tell you
    meaner.
What happens when a bug gets sucked up in a vacuum
    cleaner?

Boom Snap Clap (74, 172)

Boom snap clap boom boom snap clap snap.
Boom snap clap boom boom snap clap snap boom.
Two! Three! Warm it up!

Boom snap clap boom boom snap clap snap.
Boom snap clap boom boom snap clap snap boom.
Two! Three! Give it more now!

Tuna Fish Ice Cream (77, 173)

Tuna fish ice cream,
cauliflower cupcakes,
cookies with onions
and choc'late chips!

Picking Up a Pepperoni Pizza (78, 174)

Picking up a pepperoni pizza,
Lotsa mozzarella and lotsa meatsa.
I love a pizza pie!
Big-a bite-a pizza, me oh my!

My Name Is (79, 175)

My name is Sarah Samantha Susan Cecilia
Emmabemma Billingsley Harrington Hobb.
That's my name, and here's my friend,
and he'll tell you his name: Bob.

Do-Be-Dop (80, 176)

Doo-be-doo-be-dop-dop. Doo-be-doo-be-dop-dop.
Doo-be-doo-be-doo-be-doo-be-doo-be-doo-be-dop-dop.
Doo-be-doo-be-dop-dop. Doo-be-doo-be-dop-dop.
Doo-be-doo-be-doo-be-doo-be-doo-be-doo-be-doo. Dop!

La lo, la lo,
la lo, la-la lo.
La lo, la lo,
la lo, la lo, la lo.

Ooma. Ooma. Ooma. Ooma.
Ooma. Ooma. Ooma. Ooma.
Ooma. Ooma. Ooma. Ooma.
Ooma. Ooma. Ooma. Ooma-ma.

Shu-bah. Shu-bah, shu-bah, shu-bah, shu-bah.
Shu-bah-shu-bah, shu-bah-shu-bah, shu-ba-shu-bah, shu-
    bah.
Shu-bah. Shu-bah, shu-bah, shu-bah, shu-bah.
Shu-bah-shu-bah, shu-bah, shu-bah, shu-bah-shu-bah,
    shu-bah. Shu!

Country Band (82, 178)

I play drums in a country band.
I play drums whenever I can.
Wham! Bam!
Whompity bomp.
Wham! Bam!
Whompity, whompity bomp!

Guitar player in a country band.
I play guitar whenever I can.
Boom-ching, boom-pa ching,
boom-ching-a-ching-ching.
Boom-ching, boom-ba-joomba-joom,
ching.

I fiddle with my fiddle.
I fiddle with my fiddle.
I fiddle with my fiddle whenever I can.
I fiddle with my fiddle.
I fiddle with my fiddle.
I fiddle with my fiddle whenever I can.

I'm the singer for a country band.
I sing songs whenever I can.
Like, "My true love left me feelin' blue.
He took my heart and my pick-up, too."

I Love My Neck (84, 180)

Chorus
I love my neck. *(I love my neck.)*
Lucky for me. *(Lucky for me.)*
It sits on my collar *(It sits on my collar)*
in just the right place it should be, should be!

I love my neck. *(I love my neck.)*
Perfect design. *(Perfect design.)*
It sits on my collar. *(It sits on my collar.)*
I love how it tops off my spine, my spine!

My neck is fantastic.
It highlights my chin,
and it always looks perfect to me, to me.
It's also so handy for holding my head up
so it won't fall onto my knee, my knee.

Chorus

Emma Wants Ice Cream (85, 182)

Emma wants ice cream, so do I!
Emma wants ice cream, so do I!
Emma wants ice cream, so do I!

Oh, no! Now Emma wants (doughnuts, Tinkertoys...whatever each new leader chooses for Emma to want.)

Good Night (86, 185)

Good night.
Sleep tight.
Don't let the bed-bugs bite.
Good night.
Sleep tight.
But if they do bite,
bite them back and they won't be back tomorrow night.

Monsters in My Closet (86, 185)

Monsters in my closet.
Monsters under my bed.
Want to get those monsters and bash 'em in the head.
Then I'll get some sleep!

Dancing on a Daisy (87, 187)

Dancing on a daisy,
dainty little butterfly.
Wings whisper softly as she flutters by.
Tiptoeing on a tulip,
waltzing here and there.
A butterfly's a poem
set to music in the air.

Goop Glop (87, 187)

Goop, glop, sludge, slop.
Muddy puddles of gruesome gunk.
Sleaze! Slime! Grease! Grime!
Eww! Awful aroma of skunk.

M & Ms (88, 189)

M & Ms and a bag of Reese's Pieces.
Bubblicious Bubble Gum.
Gummy Bears. Yum, yum!

TIME SIGNATURES AND KEY SIGNATURES AT A GLANCE

A list of the songs with their time signatures and key signatures

Songs to the Tune of Old Favorites

6/8 C Bill Loves Jill
3/4 G My Bonnie Went in for a Face Lift
4/4 C Z-Y-X
3/4 F Oh, My Darling Frankensteen
3/4 C On Top of a Bald Guy
3/4 F My Bike Has a Flat Tire
4/4 C Mary Possessed a Petite Offspring of a Ewe
4/4 F A Spaceship Landed
4/4 D I Am the Very Model of a Perfect Son or Daughter
2/4 G There's a House in the Middle of the Town

Story Songs

3/4 G Boa Constrictor
4/4 C Whiffling, Waffling Will
4/4 C Victor Vacuumed
4/4 C Peas
4/4 G Alexander's Outside Eating Bugs
6/8 C Cell Phone Song
4/4 Bb Don't Wanna Be a Couch Potato
4/4 C Bill Bought a Backpack Bigger than Bill

Miscellaneous Fun

4/4 C Never Hug a Hibble
3/4 C Her Poodle Likes Noodles
3/4 F I Like Your Singin'
4/4 C Surfing Polka Band
4/4 C Impossible to Sing Song
4/4 C Ugh!
4/4 C This Is a Boring Song
4/4 F Yes!
4/4 C Snot Is Not the Proper Subject for a Song

Warm-Ups and Rounds

4/4 C Pat Picked Pepperoni Pizza
4/4 C Wiggle Your Fingers
4/4 C Never Hug an Alligator
4/4 B I've Got a Cat
4/4 Bb Ecka Booly
4/4 C Macaroni and Cheese
4/4 C Itsy Bitsy Down the Drain
4/4 C Boom Snap Clap

Songs for More than One Person

4/4 C Tuna Fish Ice Cream
4/4 C Picking up a Pepperoni Pizza
4/4 C My Name Is
4/4 C Doo-Be-Dop
4/4 C Country Band
4/4 Bb I Love My Neck
4/4 C Emma Wants Ice Cream
4/4 C Good Night and Monsters in My Closet
4/4 D Dancing on a Daisy and Goop Glop
4/4 C M & Ms

INDEX

About the Authors

Heather Stenner is a music teacher and the founder of Enthusic, a company devoted to helping young people discover the joy of music without the pressure of performance. She is a member of the National Association for Music Education and the Colorado Music Educators Association. She lives in Fort Collins, Colorado, with her husband and two young children.

Cheryl Miller Thurston is a former English and writing teacher who has written many plays, musicals, and books for teachers. She is a past winner of the Northwest Writers' Conference Children's Play Award and was a 1997 finalist for the Colorado Book Award. She lives in Loveland, Colorado, with her husband and pampered cat.

Together, Stenner and Thurston write music for the performing group Moonlighting Teachers. They are also co-authors of the musical comedy *A Hair from the Head of a Prince* and the songwriters for the "No Child Left Behind Blues" CD for teachers.

To Order More Copies of

SINGuini

Please send me _____ copies of *SINGuini*. I am enclosing $18.95 per book, plus shipping and handling ($6.00 for one book, $1.00 for each additional book). Colorado residents add 54¢ sales tax per book. Total amount: $_____.

Ship To:

Name _____

School _____
(Include only if using school address.)

Address _____

City _____ State _____ Zip Code _____

Phone _____

Method of Payment:

❑ Payment enclosed ❑ Visa/MC/Discover ❑ Purchase Order (must be attached)

Credit Card# _____Expiration Date_____

Signature _____

Cardholder Name _____

Cardholder Billing Address (if different from shipping address):

Address _____

City _____ State _____ Zip Code _____

Cottonwood Press, Inc.
**109-B Cameron Drive
Fort Collins, CO 80525**
1-800-864-4297
www.cottonwoodpress.com
**Visit web site for complete product list.
View sample pages.
Order online.
Sign up for free activity every month!**